IN CELEBRATION OF
LIGHT

Photographs from the Collection

of

Cherye R. and James F. Pierce

Honolulu Academy of Arts

FRONTISPIECE

Robert Mapplethorpe

Lucy Ferry, 1986
Platinum emulsion on linen canvas

Copyright © 2003
Honolulu Academy of Arts
900 South Beretania Street
Honolulu, Hawai'i 96814-1495
Tel: 808 532-8700
www.honoluluacademy.org

ISBN 0-937426-62-8
LCCN 2003096251

Designed and produced by Barbara Pope Book Design
Printed by Meridian Printing

Contents

Preface

Henri Cartier-Bresson

Place de l'Europe

1932/PRINTED LATER

Gelatin silver print

In Celebration of Light is the first major exhibition of photography organized by the Honolulu Academy of Arts in the past twenty years, and marks a significant turning point in our treatment of modern and contemporary art. I am deeply grateful to Cherye and Jim Pierce for sharing their treasures with the people of Hawai'i. Their collection eloquently touches on twentieth century American and European cultural history expressed in the art of master photographers. At the same time, the collection as a whole is imbued with a remarkably coherent spirit, in which we see the minds and hearts of the collectors themselves. Its bold and eclectic range speaks to the dynamic power of this medium, and to the Pierces' intense intellectual curiosity.

Among the many individuals who deserve our gratitude for their work in bringing this marvelous exhibition to fruition, I would especially like to thank George Ellis, my predecessor as the Academy's director, and Jennifer Saville, curator of Western art, who worked tirelessly on the project and was ably assisted by Natasha Roessler, curatorial assistant in the department of Western art. For the beautiful catalogue that illustrates seventy-six of the photographs in the exhibition, we thank Shuzo Uemoto, the Academy's photographer, E. John Bullard and Robert Becker for their thoughtful written contributions, and Barbara Pope, who designed this handsome volume.

Stephen Little

Director and President

Honolulu Academy of Arts

Diane Arbus

A Woman with Her Baby Monkey, New Jersey, 1971
Gelatin silver print

Foreword

E. John Bullard

The Montine McDaniel Freeman Director
New Orleans Museum of Art

It was only thirty years ago that photography first gained widespread
recognition as a fine art, with the activities of a few pioneer dealers,
private collectors, and museum curators. Now, in the first years of
the new millennium, rare, vintage photographs of the nineteenth and
twentieth centuries command hundreds of thousands of dollars each,
museums across the country regularly mount photography exhibitions
that attract record crowds, and many of the most critically praised and
avidly collected contemporary artists choose to work in the photographic medium.

In 1970 there were only a few museums with a serious commitment
to photography, the Museum of Modern Art in New York and the George
Eastman House in Rochester being the most prominent. There were
only a handful of galleries devoted exclusively to photography then,
such as the Lee Witkin Gallery and the Light Gallery in New York and
the Harry Lunn Gallery in Washington, D.C. These were soon followed
by G. Ray Hawkins in Los Angeles, Tom Halstead in Michigan, Gerhard
Sander in Washington, D.C., and Joshua Mann Pailet in New Orleans.
There were only a few reference books and artist monographs to consult
in those days. Beaumont Newhall's slim *History of Photography, from 1839
to the Present Day* was practically the only comprehensive survey and
served as an essential guide to novice collectors.

My museum's first photography purchases in the spring of 1973 were
a Walker Evans portfolio and several Ansel Adams images, including
the image (famous even then) *Moonrise, Hernandez, New Mexico*. Prices
were ridiculously low (only four hundred dollars for each Adams photograph) for works by the masters in the field. Many great twentieth-
century American photographers were then still living. Most of them

were so thrilled with the sudden critical and public attention and actual commercial sales that they were delighted to attend gallery openings. Imagine the pleasure of meeting and talking with artists like Berenice Abbott, Ansel Adams, Imogen Cunningham, Brett Weston, Barbara Morgan, André Kertész and W. Eugene Smith, now all sadly gone.

Cherye and Jim Pierce were members of the pioneering group of collectors in the 1970s who became passionately addicted to photography, buying their first images soon after their marriage in 1973. They joined a small but dedicated group—including, most famously, Sam Wagstaff, Paul Walther, and Arnold Crane—who helped bring long-overdue public recognition to an art medium that already had a rich history dating back over 135 years. It was an exciting time. There were so many discoveries to be made, reputations to be revived, histories to be written, and young photographers to be encouraged and patronized.

After 1980 the fast developing market for fine photography, spurred on by new dealers and the auction houses, was a catalyst for the discovery and availability of unique and unusual vintage material. When prices rose to thousands and tens of thousands of dollars, great examples by the most important masters began to appear on the market. Collectors quickly became aware of how rare and few in number were these treasures. In the past, most photographers had made only a handful of prints from their negatives at the time of creation. Later prints, even those made by the original artist, bring much lower prices than vintage prints. Scarcity of work by earlier masters is one factor in the now tremendous collecting interest in a select number of contemporary photographers, whose new work is produced in severely limited editions, creating an artificial rarity that commands high prices immediately.

In selecting and organizing this exhibition of 116 photographs from the Pierces' extraordinarily diverse collection, we could have taken any one of several different approaches. The Pierces themselves continually rehang their photographs in different combinations throughout their home. The works could be arranged by artist or by stylistic trends, or chronologically in a historic sequence or thematically by subject. Any of these approaches would have been valid, but for this exhibition we chose the thematic one as the best way to showcase a rich variety of works. In consultation with the Pierces, we developed seven categories arising from their personal interests: the natural environment, the urban environment, the human condition, nudes, animals, still lifes, and the modernist impulse. After selecting works in each category, we added one more category, to serve as an introduction to the rest—the iconic image. This is a group of photographs of varied subjects that are so often reproduced, so well known, and so embedded in the popular consciousness that they have achieved the status of icons, like van Gogh's paintings of sunflowers or Monet's images of water lilies.

A photograph becomes an icon when it is widely reproduced in histories of the medium, in art journals and magazines, in monographs and catalogues of the photographer's work, and in the popular press.

Spanish Village Spinner, p. 11

Sometimes the image appears first in the mass media, like W. Eugene Smith's *Spanish Village Spinner* or Robert Capa's *Loyalist Soldier, Spain*, both published in *Life* Magazine. Then, over the years, the photograph reappears in exhibitions and publications, and so becomes acknowledged as the photographer's best or most famous work. In the case of Ansel Adams's *Moonrise, Hernandez, New Mexico*, uniquely, the artist contributed to the iconic status of the image by making hundreds of prints in different sizes to fill the huge demands of collectors and dealers in the late 1970s. While it is ridiculous to think that an artist's entire career can be summed up by one or two or even a dozen works, particularly since most photographers make thousands of images over a lifetime, these iconic images have become fixed in the public mind when thinking of these artists. Yet these photographs can still amaze and delight us even after so many viewings. Irving Penn's *Cuzco Children*, tiny figures isolated against a wrinkled canvas backdrop, remain forever dignified, enchanting, and sad. The extraordinary beauty of

Magnolia Blossom, p. 5

Imogen Cunningham's *Magnolia Blossom*, with its rich tonal range, is more perfect than any real flower. Part of the eternal perfection of such an image is its black and white composition, which separates it from perceived reality. Nearly all the great photographers of the first three-quarters of the twentieth century worked exclusively in black and white. This classic palette is preferred by Cherye and Jim Pierce, who have acquired few color photographs for their collection.

The natural environment has attracted photographers since the invention of the medium. Many of America's greatest nineteenth-century photographers specialized in landscapes. These images were often made while the photographers were accompanying government survey teams documenting the territory west of the Mississippi. If photography had been invented in their day, Lewis and Clark would surely have taken a photographer with them in 1804 on their journey of exploration. The sense of discovering a new world of natural wonders, seen in the work of such pioneers as Carleton Watkins and William Henry Jackson, finds its ultimate expression in Ansel Adams's landscapes, as well as those of Edward and Brett Weston and others.

Since many great photographers live and work in cities, particularly New York, the urban environment has been an important subject in its own right. Alfred Stieglitz's *Flatiron Building* is a historic document of an early New York skyscraper, while also capturing the excitement of the human-built environment. The architectural richness of the city is celebrated by many photographers in this exhibition, including Berenice Abbott, Max Yavno, and Sheila Metzner.

The Pierces are often attracted to photographs with a humorous slant. Many of these amusing images depict the human condition, a favorite subject of artists through time. While photographers like Arnold Newman and August Sander create great formal portraits, the instantaneous nature of photography, as exemplified by Henri Cartier-Bresson's quest for the "decisive moment," gives this medium a unique advantage over painting and sculpture. The photographer has the ability to capture fleeting human expressions in unposed, natural situations, which express the arbitrary, accidental nature of life. A marvelous

moment of exuberance is perfectly caught in Valerie Shaff's *Carlo Aloft*, while the pathos of war is graphically depicted in Don McCullin's *Shell Shocked Man, Hue, Vietnam*.

The unclothed, naked body is the most basic aspect of the human condition, and the Pierces have collected a rich array of nudes. Nearly all are female and quite sensuous. While a few are documentary in nature, such as Bellocq's and Brassaï's studies of prostitutes, others are more stylized compositions, often focusing on just a portion of

the body. Edward Maxey's large, elegant *Maryanne* displays a nearly abstract quality without a face to give it any individuality. One of the great pleasures in this section of the exhibition is the glorious nude of Hawai'i-based Franco Salmoiraghi, whose figure reflects the erotic and lush qualities of the islands themselves.

Photographs of animals, both wild and domestic, and still life

Pelican, p. 71
Sleeping Swan, p. 75

A Woman with Her Baby
Monkey, New Jersey, p. viii

compositions, both simple and elaborate, have long been favorites of the Pierces. Among the animal studies are some that focus on the subject by itself, often in close-up detail. The exhibition includes a strong selection of such compositions, such as Bettina Rheims's *Pelican*, a stuffed museum specimen, and Keith Carter's exquisite *Sleeping Swan*. Others show an animal with a person, expressing that often tender, complex relationship of people with their pets. Diane Arbus's *A Woman with Her Baby Monkey, New Jersey* is a particularly poignant and strong example; another is the even more bizarre *Snowy the Mouse Man, Cambridge* by Don McCullin.

Still lifes were produced by some of the earlier photographers, such as Louis Jacques Daguerre and William Fox Talbot, because the long exposure time then needed made an inanimate composition the perfect subject. Nearly all the still lifes in the Pierce collection are botanicals. Many are close-ups that project the viewer into the heart of a flower, like Ron van Dongen's *Dahlia, "Jessie G.,"* and the already-mentioned

Magnolia Blossom, p. 5

Magnolia Blossom of Imogen Cunningham. Others are broader in scale, such as the artfully arranged, elegant compositions of Robert Mapplethorpe and David Halliday.

Although photography is often considered to be the most realistic artistic medium, the modernist impulse in twentieth-century art found some of its greatest expressions in photography, particularly in abstraction and surrealism. Sometimes these images are the result of the special nature of the camera, which produces close-ups (even microscopic), wide angles, bird's-eye and fish-eye views, and multiple exposures, giving photographers the means to develop a vocabulary unique to their medium. Abstraction in the Pierce collection is varied in style,

Leaf Pattern, p. 96

ranging from Cunningham's *Leaf Pattern* and Paul Strand's *Abstraction, Porch Shadows, Twin Lakes, Connecticut* to Aaron Siskind's *Jerome, Arizona*. Surrealism is a style of continuing fascination for photographers, ranging here from the poetic manipulations of Jerry N. Uelsmann to the macabre tableaus of Joel Peter Witkin.

Altogether this selection of works from the Pierce's collection presents the viewer with a rich diversity of images by nearly one hundred of the most accomplished photographic masters of the past century. This exhibition also is a testimony to this couple's joint passion and persistence in assembling a collection of great distinction and beauty.

Franco Salmoiraghi

Cherye and Jim Pierce, New Orleans, 1999
Gelatin silver print

Introduction

Cherye and Jim Pierce

Collecting photography has been a joy for us, and we are pleased to share a part of our collection with you. Our search for photographs began thirty years ago, shortly after our marriage, and has served as a bond of common interest in our relationship. When we travel, we almost always go to galleries and museums, sometimes casually wandering through a show, at other times exploring in depth and purchasing one or more pieces to add to our collection. Sometimes we seek out a specific work. We buy for each other, as a way to celebrate birthdays, anniversaries, and other special occasions.

There have been many memorable moments over the years, as we have acquired photographs. Cherye watched as two children wandered into a Diane Arbus show in a gallery in New Orleans. They stopped in front of a photograph that was taken at a nudist resort, pointed, laughed, and walked out the door. There was Jim's discovery of a vintage Imogen Cunningham photograph in an antique shop in San Francisco. There followed some bargaining about the price. There was much anxiety as he walked around the block, fearing that someone else might buy it. It was still there on his return, and the shop owner took two hundred dollars off the far-below-market price.

We have met many photographers over the years, including the eccentric, sadly infirm Clarence John Laughlin, and have received holiday cards with original photos from Rod Cook. Jim spent an afternoon with Franco Salmoiraghi in the darkroom, dodging, burning, and toning a photograph until that "perfect" print was achieved, a process that enhanced his appreciation of photography. Cherye, in her trips to New Orleans, became friends with gallery owner Joshua Mann Pailet. He shared his latest finds, and his gallery shows featured a vast array of masterworks available in those early days of collecting. His knowledge and gallery stimulated her interest and offered opportunities to meet photographers Joyce Tenneson, Josephine Sacabo, and David Halliday. There was a wonderful dinner with Maggi Weston and her photographer-husband Rod Dresser, listening to anecdotes about Ansel Adams and other renowned photographers with whom they had had contact in the very early days of art photography. We could fill pages recounting the rich experiences that collecting photography has offered us.

We are grateful to the many gallery owners, curators, and photographers who have been a part of our journey through the years. We are especially grateful to Jennifer Saville, curator of Western art at the Honolulu Academy of Arts, George Ellis, past director of the Academy, Stephen Little, the Academy's current director, and John Bullard, director of the New Orleans Museum of Art, for their encouragement and assistance in preparing this exhibition. There are many others who have offered their opinions, advice, and help, and to them also we express our thanks.

Collecting photography is fun. It is an evolving, contemporary medium. One can still collect prints by nineteenth- and twentieth-century "masters" of photography, though these are less easily available as they become part of museum, corporate, and established private collections. However, there are many actively working photographers, including those with established reputations and many emerging, innovative photographers. One can find photographs available for hundreds of thousands of dollars and wonderful images for less than a thousand dollars. There are ample opportunities to meet collectors, gallery owners, museum photography curators, and photographers themselves. Collectors are often willing to share and talk about their collections. Gallery owners are a valuable source for education. Curators can make arrangements for collectors to view special collections and to consult their extensive library resources. The photographers, uniquely in touch with life, are often available and interested in meeting the people who collect their work. We hope that you will experience a bit of what we have enjoyed as you view the beauty, emotion, and humor captured by the artists in their work.

We invite you to take pleasure in the exhibition as a celebration of light—the essence of photography.

A Few Photographs from the Pierce Collection

Robert Becker

A Pair

Thirty years and several hundred pictures compose the Pierce collection; 116 of the photographs are in the current exhibition. I asked Cherye and Jim Pierce to pick their individual favorites. (Judging by the way they talk about their collection, they love almost everything they own to a lesser or greater degree. How could they not? Cherye also named one picture she doesn't own but wants—Edward Steichen's portrait of Gloria Swanson from 1924. So the fire still burns.) Neither hesitated in answering the question.

Cherye chose Irving Penn's slightly haunting *Cuzco Children*. It's also titled, variously, *Mountain Children* or *Brother and Sister*. Penn took the picture at a pivotal moment in his career, as he moved from photographing artists to becoming one himself. Established already with Condé Nast, shooting portraits and fashion, the thirty-one-year-old photographer, while on location in Lima, Peru, for *Vogue* Magazine, left the city and headed to Cuzco for Christmas. Cuzco was "a town I had . . . a hunch about," he wrote. "I hungered to begin photographing its people the moment I set eyes on them. . . . And then, by incredible providence, there in the center of the town was a daylight studio! A Victorian leftover, one broad wall of light to the north, a stone floor, a painted cloth backdrop."[1] The backdrop eliminated any context; it's only you and two ragged children looking across the distance right at each other. The picture's subjects probably seemed exotic to an audience in 1948. Penn brought back to New York his fascinating bag, much as a *National Geographic* photographer might. Fifty years later we are more worldly. Shorn by time of its foreignness, the art of the picture has instead moved to the foreground, pulled by the plaza's flagstones and Penn's broad vision.

André Kertész

At the Animal Market, Quai St. Michel, Paris (Boy with Puppy), 1927–1928
Gelatin silver print

Jim Pierce said his favorite is *At the Animal Market, Quai St. Michel, Paris (Boy with Puppy)* by André Kertész, another picture of a child. No picture in the collection carries with it as much pathos or tension. We expect boys and puppies to be cute, a charming subject. But Kertész offers something else: menace, vulnerability, pride, love, and a dozen questions. *Boy with Puppy* is a found image, a "street photograph," as opposed to a studio picture. Kertész no doubt guided the little boy a little, but it took a practiced eye to see the possibility and then frame it just so. The French critic and author Roland Barthes once remarked that this was an important image to him as well.

Roland Barthes

I see photographs everywhere, like everyone else, nowadays; they come from the world to me, without my asking; they are only "images," their mode of appearance is heterogeneous. Yet, among those which had been selected, evaluated, approved, collected in albums or magazines and which had thereby passed through the filter of culture, I realized that some provoked tiny jubilations, as if they referred to a stilled center, an erotic or lacerating value buried in myself . . . and that others, on the contrary, were so indifferent to me that by dint of seeing them multiply, like some weed, I felt a kind of aversion toward them, even of irritation: there are moments when I detest Photographs. . . .[2]

Roland Barthes from *Camera Lucida*

History

By pulling just nine of the photographers in the Pierce collection out of line, a snapshot history of twentieth-century American photography takes shape—a bite-sized primer. It begins with Alfred Stieglitz in 1902 and ends with Robert Mapplethorpe in 1986. Though photography's march is relatively short compared with thousands of years of painting, sculpture, architecture, or theater—its most rudimentary forms were only invented in 1826 and 1839—distinct demarcations nonetheless exist in its technical and philosophical evolution, as well as in the general acceptance of the medium as a legitimate art form. There are dozens of photographers whose names might be writ large in any history of the medium, a number of whom are represented in the Pierce collection. These nine, however, best suit the purpose.

Chronologically Stieglitz comes first, but he also comes first in stature by virtue of the enormous contributions he made as an artist and in his spirited promotion of photography and modern art in America. Stieglitz is the beginning of a twentieth-century time line, but he is also the bridge from art's *ancien régime* to today. Born at the end of the Civil War, he learned photography in Germany when it was taught as a discipline of chemistry rather than art. (Mapplethorpe, a century later, studied photography in art school.) His earliest works, dating from the 1880s and 1890s, illustrate the *fin-de-siècle*—horses, buggies, top hats, and all—and are part of its artistic tradition of fuzzy pictorialism. Around 1900, however, as though waking up to an electric alarm clock, Stieglitz opened his eyes to the hard edges, sharp contrasts, and loaded imagery of modernism, capturing it through his lens and in his darkroom. From then on this new sensibility was part of everything he did: He made forty years' worth of ground-breaking pictures, including *The Steerage* of 1907 and the decades-long portrait series of his wife Georgia O'Keeffe; he founded *Camera Work* Magazine; and he established the galleries "291" and later An American Place in New York City, each exhibiting work by significant artists from Picasso to O'Keeffe. Stieglitz is credited with being the first dealer ever to put up a show of modern art in the United States. Not only did he help invent American modern art, he loudly let the public know about it.

Flatiron Building, p. 3

Flatiron Building from the Pierce collection was made by Stieglitz just at that moment when his vision and understanding coalesced. He shot it in 1903, the year the structure, one of New York's first skyscrapers, was completed. The picture is a celebration of a distinct symbol of architectural and engineering advancement; to anyone in that era the eccentric, triangular building manifested all the potential of a new epoch. (So compelling was it that Steichen photographed it himself in 1904, later showing the pictures at Stieglitz's "291"; Alvin Langdon Coburn shot it in 1912; and Berenice Abbott did the same for her study of New York in the early 1930s.) But Stieglitz was asking more of his camera than simply to record the sight, and more of the subject than just architectural wonder. As René Magritte put it, "*Ceci n'est pas une pipe.*" For Stieglitz the Flatiron was a tool for his art: the building, like the tree in the foreground with snow packed into its crotch, and the horizontal, slightly arced row of park benches at the bottom of the image, all served him much more with their geometric forms and directing lines than as illustrations of a particularly interesting view. The mist in the air (exaggerated in the way Stieglitz printed the picture) blurs the objects, further divorcing them from what they were in the world versus what they become in his picture. *Flatiron Building* is a conceptually astute comment, and an early experiment in abstraction.

Alfred Stieglitz left two more significant gifts beyond his own work that advanced the medium. He was the first in America to treat photography—regard it, hang it, sell it, and collect it—as fine art. "Mysterious are the ways of art history," Walker Evans, another of the century's master photographers, observed in the 1960s. "There is a groundswell, if not a wave, of photography at this time, and it may perhaps be traced to the life work, arresting still, of one man: Alfred Stieglitz."[3] And in 1933 Stieglitz gave his own large collection of photographs to the Metropolitan Museum of Art in New York, thus partly founding the Met's collection; he was breaking new ground again, this time by pushing photography through the door of a major institution.

Paul Strand is represented in the Pierce collection with *Abstraction, Porch Shadows, Twin Lakes, Connecticut* of 1916. Strand, in making fifty years' worth of original pictures, sits right next to his mentor Alfred Stieglitz in the pantheon of American photographers. (The Museum of Modern Art in New York gave its first one-person show of photography to Strand in 1945.) Somewhat of a child prodigy, he showed and sold photographs in his early twenties, many of which still hold up as masterpieces. His most famous image might be *Blind Woman* of 1917, a startling street picture inspired by his teacher at the School of Ethical Culture in New York, Lewis Hines; another might be *Rebecca's Hands* or other images from the ongoing portrait series he began of his wife in 1920, three years after Stieglitz started shooting O'Keeffe. Or perhaps it is *Toadstool and Grasses, Georgetown, Maine*, a still life from 1928, or the portrait called *Young Boy* from his work of the early 1950s for a book titled *La France de profil*. Strand was remarkably enduring and varied in his genius, and his prints are in every major museum collection in the country.

Porch Shadows is part of a body of work Strand made on a vacation trip to the New England countryside. There he experimented with eliminating all references to the original source of images, focusing entirely on abstract forms. In a sense he took to the extreme what Stieglitz hinted at in *Flatiron Building*. Other shots from the same session—one in the collection of the Metropolitan Museum, for instance—are titled simply *Abstraction, Twin Lakes, Connecticut*, with no mention of where or how Strand found the semi-oval, the crisp triangle, or the comb-tooth pattern. His source is revealed in the name of the Pierces' print, which is our only real clue that we are looking at shadows thrown one afternoon by a porch roof and railing balusters, and a table top. In the series he accomplished what many artists were trying to achieve in all media at that time: images that weren't *of* anything, that didn't illustrate or represent something, but simply were what they were, in this case a photograph. Interestingly, the image owned by the Met is separated from the Pierces' by just a few moments in time, as proved by the lengthening of the shadows across the table.

Imogen Cunningham found the perfect marriage between abstraction and representation in the petals, leaves, stems, and stamens of plants. By pushing her lens right up to her subject, she turned one thing into another like an alchemist. She did it with nudes, too. Cunningham learned the basics of photography, as Stieglitz did, in a chemistry class; she refined her technique and practiced making platinum prints while assisting Edward S. Curtis in his darkroom. Then, while studying at the University of Washington in the early 1900s, Cunningham did part-time work for the botany department, making slides for the professors. In this unlikely laboratory she must have found what would transform her craft into her art. That understanding, that sensation—which extended into her portrait photography—made her one of the pioneers and masters of modernism on the West Coast. And it drew her into an alliance of like-minded photographers in San Francisco, including Ansel Adams, who called themselves the "f/64 Group."

A few others saw what Cunningham saw in plants, around the same time she saw it, including Strand, and many more have since used flora as subjects (as is well represented in the Pierce collection). But Imogen Cunningham led the way and perfected the genre from the start. The sharp, serrated edges in *Leaf Pattern* of 1929 pull the eye down like mountain streams rushing to a river. "Cunningham was less interested in what the plant was than in what else it might become under pressure," wrote John Szarkowski, director emeritus of photography at the Museum of Modern Art.[4] The Pierces' *Magnolia Blossom*, from 1925, her most famous plant image, has all the weight and mass of a Rodin

Leaf Pattern, p. 96

Magnolia Blossom, p. 5

bronze, while retaining a tissue-paper quality composed simply of light and air.

Ansel Adams was given a print of *Magnolia Blossom* by a friend. He called it "one of the most beautiful photographs I have ever owned." Cunningham and Adams didn't always get along personally, however. Adams believed it was because Cunningham disapproved of his own commercialism and felt that he had turned his back on his art by taking advertising jobs. He also thought "Imogen's blood was three percent acetic acid."[5]

Walker Evans lauded what Alfred Stieglitz had done for the recognition of photography, but he also turned up his nose at what he called Stieglitz's "artsicraftsiness." "The real thing that I'm talking about has purity and a certain severity, rigor, or simplicity, directness, clarity, and it is without artistic pretension."[6] Evans was from a new generation, one born in the twentieth century, that took skyscrapers for granted. Enamored of Strand's street photography, he eschewed, however, Strand's brilliant abstractions just as he dismissed much of Stieglitz's work. "The abstract games that had entranced and delighted most adventurous photographers during the decade of the twenties," wrote Szarkowski, "had lost much of their charm by the early thirties."[7]

Evans may not have intended his arresting documentary photographs as artistic statements, or maybe he just claimed in writing what he thought to be higher ground. He honestly craved an aesthetic purged of self-conscious conceit. It's difficult today, though, not to see an artist's eye and hand in a picture like *Lunchroom Buddies, New York City* (1931). At face value the image is indeed a stripped-down document relating unencumbered facts like what people ate, how they dressed, what New York City looked like, even something about friendship. We know from the date of the picture that the Great Depression was careening through American lives at that very moment. This is where Evans, like Walt Whitman, saw his poetry. On this level *Lunchroom Buddies* is accessible picture-taking by Evans; work in and of a vernacular that hints at the snaps taken by every American with a Brownie; work not aimed at an elite art world audience. But the formal qualities of the picture, the lines and shapes that pull us around the image and then settle—specifically, the diner's railing mimicked by the lean of the

Walker Evans
Lunchroom Buddies,
New York City, 1931
Gelatin silver print

counterman and the tilt of his hat, the round light over his head like
the dot above the letter *i* — ultimately reveal the magic that in the end
defines this as a picture belonging on a museum wall. This is purely
high art as passed on from Stieglitz and Strand and everyone else
whose work Evans looked at as he decided to be a photographer.
Lunchroom Buddies is as Evans wished, simple and clean as a picture
ever can be, but it was no accident.

　　The deeper conceptual gulf between Evans's work and the abstractions and still lifes of the older generation has more to do with the fundamental nature of the medium. A photograph is what's left over from an actual moment in time frozen by the camera's shutter. Evans's pictures call attention to this fact. It's present in all the work he did in New York in the late 1920s and 1930s, in the South in the mid-1930s for the government-sponsored Farm Security Administration, and in his collaboration with James Agee, *Let Us Now Praise Famous Men*. Of course, it is there to some degree in all photography: we know that an hour after Cunningham finished with the magnolia blossom, it turned brown and withered. We become aware of time in Strand's shadow abstractions when by happenstance two or three pictures from the same shoot are lined up in chronological order; Stieglitz's original prints, as modern as they were, are now yellowed or faded. In documentary photography, however, time is explicit rather than implicit. *Lunchroom Buddies* is of a concrete moment long ago; as Barthes would doubtless point out, these two friends are now both dead or very, very old. Evans's documentary pictures emphasize this important distinction, which is unique to photography and which separates it from painting: what's in a photograph actually happened. To some extent photographic still lifes hide this truth.

Evans and Ansel Adams were a continent apart in their work and personalities, yet both are integral to photography's history. Evans, the charming but aloof, slightly bent eastern urbanite, dedicated his career to documenting characters who peopled the American landscape. He later taught photography at Yale. Though his photographs of Depression victims and sharecroppers in the deep South churn up social conscience, he insisted they were apolitical. Adams was from San Francisco and was somewhat awkward and odd looking, the latter partly the result of having broken his nose during the earthquake of 1906. Antithetical to Evans, Adams found his own lifelong artistic question, and its answer, alone in the emptiness of the wilderness. While Evans photographed people, Adams photographed their absence. Adams was also tremendously famous, and his work became popular on a scale no other photographs have ever achieved before or since. He received the Presidential Medal of Freedom from Jimmy Carter; this acceptability to the establishment only stressed his separateness from the art world. He appeared in a television commercial for Datsun (to promote conservation), and sold one of his snow-covered mountain images to Hills Brothers in 1968 for their coffee cans. Imogen Cunningham said what many artists were probably thinking when she sent Adams one of the cans with a marijuana plant growing from it.[8]

Adams did with the American landscape what Evans did with its people, and then some. Evans picked out from the great population a few representative faces and moments that revealed broader truths about the nation and humanity. Adams, also using a box camera, framed representative fragments of a heretofore visually and conceptually indigestible vastness and grandeur, and did so, miraculously, without limiting its majesty.

There is an enormous amount to be said of Adams's technical prowess: his shrewdness at editing, his superb deftness at making prints. Important as this is, it's secondary in his story. Ansel Adams had the yearning. It came in part from the love affair he started with landscape at Yosemite Park in 1916, on his first trip there when he was fourteen years old and carried a Brownie. For the rest of his life he hiked, camped, and explored, living in the mountains for months at a time. Like Thoreau on Walden Pond a century before, Adams had transcendent experiences out there. Sometimes, especially in his work of the 1930s and 1940s, that transcendence illuminates his pictures: this is what makes him an important artist. *Moonrise, Hernandez, New Mexico*, of 1941, a picture in the Pierce collection, not only illustrates an extraordinary moment and place—the little church, the graveyard, the three-quarters moon, the awful black sky—it offers us something of what Adams understood in his soul when he took the picture and later printed it.

Yousuf Karsh and Arnold Newman don't have quite the historical cachet of Strand, Adams, or the others in this survey, but their exquisite pictures represent in the Pierce collection an essential element in photography's time line and in the American psyche. They were both first-rate celebrity portrait photographers. (Karsh was a naturalized Canadian born in Armenia, so again the boundaries of the story are stretched to accommodate his inclusion.) By mid-century when they made these two pictures—Newman, a portrait of Igor Stravinsky from 1946, and Karsh, one of Georgia O'Keeffe from 1956—mass media equaled other postwar industries in production, cranking out overnight success and instant icons. The true audience for photography then, which remains the case today, was not gallery or museum patrons but magazine subscribers. (Every photographer in this abbreviated history, other than Stieglitz, worked for the large-circulation print media during his or her career.) One of the biggest segments of the photography profession itself, if not the biggest, was celebrity reporting. Newman and Karsh were at the top of their field; neither needed to peep over a wall for the shot. Karsh photographed Ernest Hemingway, Dwight Eisenhower, Humphrey Bogart, Pablo Picasso, Frank Lloyd Wright, Laurence Olivier, J. Paul Getty, Albert Einstein, George Bernard Shaw, and Queen Elizabeth II. A portrait of a cross but resolute Winston Churchill taken in 1941, seconds after Karsh reached out and took a cigar away from him, made Karsh's career. Wright and Eisenhower also sat for Newman, as did Picasso in the same year (1954) he sat for Karsh. O'Keeffe and Stieglitz posed together for Newman in 1944, two years before Stieglitz died; Marilyn Monroe, Willem de Kooning, Eugene O'Neill, and Yasuo Kuniyoshi were also photographed by him.

Newman's portrait of Stravinsky is two photographs in one. There is the picture of the great composer seated by his instrument; the piano dwarfs Stravinsky in the image, as perhaps Newman perceived his musical gift dwarfed his person. Or maybe Newman the artist was

Arnold Newman
Igor Stravinsky,
1946/PRINTED LATER
Gelatin silver print

Yousuf Karsh

Georgia O'Keeffe, 1956/PRINTED LATER
Gelatin silver print

simply fascinated by the outline of the piano's black lid against a light background, an organic abstract form like those in paintings by Barnett Newman and others made around the same time. Arnold Newman is still working in his late eighties, the only photographer mentioned in this survey who's still alive.

Karsh caught O'Keeffe in her own element, at home in the New Mexico desert; the arid swirl of plaster, the grain of the parched stump, the antlers of an elk are ingredients that might have been in one of her paintings and that here rhyme with her hair and hands and the lines in her face. A vertical blade of sunshine and the room's window-pane punctuate the image. Karsh was a John Trumbull of twentieth-century photography: precise, nearly perfect, quite dry.

A Woman with Her Baby Monkey, New Jersey, p. viii

Where Karsh and Newman found universal elegance in their accomplished subjects, Diane Arbus sought to photograph the unsettling side of humanity, which actually might be a more universally relevant (and appealing) theme. The Pierces own a print of *A Woman with Her Baby Monkey, New Jersey*, from 1971, a photograph she took to illustrate "Assignment: Love" for the Life Library of Photography. It was one of Arbus's last jobs before she committed suicide. Like nearly all of her work, instead of it soothing with some expressed beauty, this picture is excruciatingly uncomfortable to spend time with. We're shoved right up to the couple, an insinuation that the room is narrow and claustrophobic and that we are stuck in this company. The figures in the portrait are right of center, giving a great deal of emphasis to a small window and its broken venetian blind, the tacky, ill-fitting slip-cover on a fringed sofa, and the smudges and fingerprints on the fake wood paneling. The woman, as photographed by Arbus, has a large head and her face is slightly out of focus, as in many everyday family photos. Her body looks inordinately thin and her bony, frail arms seem jarringly similar to the arms of the monkey in her lap. To make matters worse, the monkey is dressed like a human baby, and the woman's trousers are too short. "I do feel I have some slight corner on something about the quality of things," Arbus said the year she made the picture. "I mean it's very subtle and a little embarrassing to me, but I really believe there are things which nobody would see unless I photographed them."[9] This one is Arbus's take on the classical subject of Madonna and Child; the flash even leaves a slight halo behind the woman's head. Arbus, like each of the other photographers spoken of here, invented a unique, idiosyncratic, completely recognizable language.

Some of Arbus's best known images—freaks and midgets, lunatics and nudists and odd children—were photographed outdoors. One of the dividends in this picture is that it was shot inside. Because she worked here with a backdrop, the photographer's signature, a sort of footprint, is left behind in the sheen of the flash on the wall (the halo), and in the reflection on the woman's boots. It tells us that Diane Arbus and her camera were there that day.

Like an Arbus, there is no mistaking one of Robert Mapplethorpe's pictures. All of them possess a certain cut, like the best Savile Row suit, crisp and perfectly tailored, never a wrinkle. This is the case whether it is a portrait of, say, an artist like Andy Warhol or Francesco Clemente, or a ten-inch penis. Mapplethorpe was an avowed perfectionist; he brushed all serendipity and potential accident, the hallmark of photographers like Arbus and Evans, out of the process. He demanded control in his studio; many of his photographs, particularly the classical nudes and posed sadomasochistic pairings, depict metaphors for that control.

Mapplethorpe, more than any other artist in the Pierce collection, represents the extraordinary impact of photography at the end of the twentieth century. That his work could rile a national politician (Jesse Helms) to such a degree that he would revile it on the floor of the U.S. Senate and call for its censorship, or that the director of a Cincinnati art museum would actually be arrested in recent years by local police and put on trial for obscenity for exhibiting Mapplethorpe's sexually explicit pictures, reveals just how much power resides within the young medium. (The director was acquitted, Helms has finally retired, and many of Mapplethorpe's images are easily found on the Internet or for sale in art galleries.) Photographs made as art and as social commentary, as some of Mapplethorpe's were, have the fantastic potential to polarize an entire society and even edge some of its stubborn thinking slightly forward.

The pictures in the Pierce collection show the art of Mapplethorpe free of the controversy. In her portrait, Lucy Ferry, the musician Brian Ferry's wife, is treated by the photographer much the way that a saint's image might be handled by a painter making an icon. Dead still and meditative, she gently emerges from the dark background serenely looking into the distance, her lovely head supported in her hands and arms like a priceless relic. Mapplethorpe actually made this platinum print on linen, accentuating its connection to painting and his conjecture that his picture is a unique object, as opposed to a mass-produced image. Like this one, most of Mapplethorpe's portraits have the inanimate quality of a still life. Conversely, some of his still lifes have the biographical details of a portrait. *Allium and Bird of Paradise* (1979), a second Mapplethorpe belonging to the Pierces, is a simple arrangement of two flowers. Here the prickly spikes of a bird of paradise below an ovoid allium are isolated against a monochrome background, just as he photographed many of his human subjects. Mapplethorpe winks at artificial perspective (an invention that revolutionized painting) with a rectangular table in the foreground of the picture plane. These photographs, like so much of Mapplethorpe's work, share an eerie grace, like a classical requiem. "He was an aesthete," wrote Luc Sante of Mapplethorpe, "who saw beauty in his subjects and sought to make this beauty manifest."[10] This same thing could have been said about Stieglitz. So we've come full circle.

Allium and Bird of Paradise,
p. 88

Looking

The luxury in writing about art is the unfettered time given you in privacy to quietly look and look at single works. In the 1980s, when on the staff of Andy Warhol's *Interview* Magazine, I was regularly invited to press previews at the Metropolitan Museum of Art and the Museum of Modern Art in New York, as well as dozens of other institutions around the country and abroad. The museum people left us virtually alone at these functions, in the large rooms filled with precious objects: no crowds, no hurry. (This is a pleasure museum staff must have every day.) Other days I spent long afternoons in artists' studios staring, talking, and staring some more. Of course, the ideal to me is to own the works, like the Dukes of Devonshire or Cherye and Jim Pierce: to have a small, favorite piece tucked in a desk drawer, folios stacked in a closet, familiar, timeless masterpieces hung cheek by jowl on a staircase wall. For a while last May, the Honolulu Academy of Arts gave me the next best thing, a comfortable seat at a table in a back office. From there I saw, at my own pace, and held in my hands, the 116 pictures in this exhibition, mostly unframed prints at that juncture. I happily rolled around in the collection for ten days.

In Praise of Small Things

James Pitts used the smallest format for the biggest subject. *World Trade Center through Branches* (1998) is just 2⅛ inches by 2¹⁄₁₆ inches, around the size of a large denomination postage stamp. A private, intimate revery, of the building and his own craftsmanship, he couldn't have made it any differently.

This picture is one of six such jewels in the Pierce collection. Part of the same tradition as miniature portrait painting, these tiny photographs have a delicacy that requires a commitment on a par with reading poetry. For instance, there are depths in Mark Citret's *Quince* of 1997 (4½ inches by 4 inches) to entirely disappear into. He illuminated the concavity of the fruit and convexity of the leaves with a spritz of silky narrative glow; the silver print is so fine, the fuzz on the quince's skin stands on end.

Brett Weston's *Furniture Detail* of 1925 (4½ inches by 3⅜ inches) is like an old friend. A photograph can do this, can distill nostalgia. Its knots and splits, its insistence of pattern, the gentle cant of picture plane, are all pleasantly familiar.

The same is true for the sloped stone steps centuries passed in André Kertész's exquisite *Untitled (Doorway, Budapest)* of 1924 (1½ inches by 2 inches). It's a well-worn path because the way in is irresistible, the trap smartly laid.

Paul Outerbridge shot his classical little study *Untitled (Compote with Fruit)* of 1922 (4½ inches by 3⅜ inches) from above and a little to the side. The spheres in his composition—apples and oranges, the bowl and its base—float above a horizon in rich tones and a perfect light borrowed from Cézanne.

And Minor White called his small seascape *Song without Words #2* (c. 1947). He printed the image just 3⅜ inches by 4½ inches, so that to hear this score for waves and moonlight, you have to stop everything else and look very carefully.

"What it produces in me . . . ," wrote Barthes, "is something more like an internal agitation, an excitement, a certain labor too, the pressure of the unspeakable which wants to be spoken."[11]

Notes

1. Penn, *Passage*, p. 58.

2. Barthes, *Camera Lucida*, p. 16.

3. Walker Evans, *Photography*, p. 1, downloaded 23 May 2003 from: www.masters-of-photography.com/E/evans_articles2.html

4. Szarkowski, *Looking at Photography*, p. 100.

5. Judy Dater, *Imogen Cunningham: A Portrait*, p. 3, downloaded 12 May 2003 from: www.masters-of-photography.com/C/cunningham/cunningham_articles3.html

6. Capa et al., *International Center of Photography Encyclopedia of Photography*, p. 178.

7. Szarkowski, *Looking at Photography*, p. 116.

8. Dater, *Imogen Cunningham: A Portrait*, p. 3.

9. Arbus and Israel, eds., *Diane Arbus*, p. 15.

10. Sante, "Unexamined Life," p. 2.

11. Barthes, *Camera Lucida*, p. 19.

Select Bibliography

Alfred Stieglitz. Koln: Koneman Verlags and Aperture Foundation, 1997.

Arbus, Doon, and Marvin Israel, editors. *Diane Arbus*. New York: Aperture Foundation, 1972.

Barthes, Roland. *Camera Lucida: Reflections on Photography*. Translated by Richard Howard. New York: Hill and Wang, 1981.

A Book of Photographs from the Collection of Sam Wagstaff. New York: Gray Press, 1978.

Capa, Cornell, et al. *International Center of Photography Encyclopedia of Photography*. New York: Pound Press/Crown Publishers, 1984.

Penn, Irving. *Passage: A Work Record*. New York: Alfred A. Knopf and Callaway, 1991.

A Personal View: Photography in the Collection of Paul F. Walter. New York: Museum of Modern Art, 1985.

Sante, Luc. "The Unexamined Life." *New York Review of Books* 42, no. 18 (16 November 1995). Downloaded 23 June 2003 from: www.nybooks.com/articles/1726

Szarkowski, John. *Ansel Adams at 100*. Boston: Little, Brown and Company, 2001.

Szarkowski, John. *Looking at Photography: 100 Pictures from the Collection of the Museum of Modern Art*. New York: Museum of Modern Art, 1973.

Walther, Thomas. *Other Pictures*. Santa Fe: Twin Palms Publishers, 2000.

The Iconic Image

Alfred Stieglitz

Flatiron Building, 1903
Large-format photogravure

Edward Steichen

Cheruit Gown, 1927
Gelatin silver print

Imogen Cunningham

Magnolia Blossom, 1925
Gelatin silver print

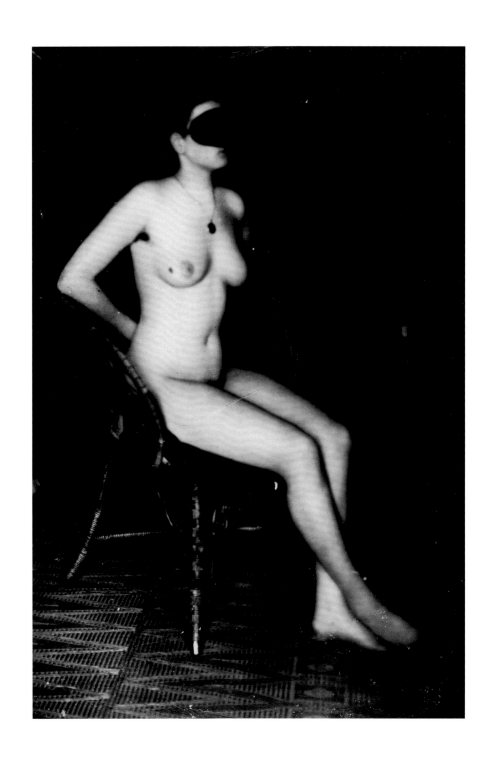

Edward J. Bellocq

Untitled (Seated Prostitute Wearing Mask), CIRCA 1912
Gelatin silver print

Lotte Johanna Jacobi

Head of a Dancer, Berlin, CIRCA 1929/PRINTED LATER
Gelatin silver print

Robert Doisneau

Le Regard Oblique (Sidelong Glance), 1948/1981
Gelatin silver print

Brassaï (Gyula Halasz)
Bijou au Bar de la Lune, Paris (Miss Diamonds), 1932/PRINTED LATER
Gelatin silver print

Barbara Morgan

Martha Graham, Letter to the World, 1940/1972
Gelatin silver print

Philippe Halsmann
Marilyn Monroe (Life Cover Variant), 1954
Gelatin silver print

Berenice Abbott

New York at Night, 1932/1960s–1970s
Gelatin silver print

The Natural Environment

Wright Morris
House in Winter, near Lincoln, Nebraska, 1941/PRINTED LATER
Gelatin silver print

Pentti Sammallahti

Solovki, White Sea, Russia, 1992
Gelatin silver print

Brett Weston

Canal, Holland, 1973
Gelatin silver print

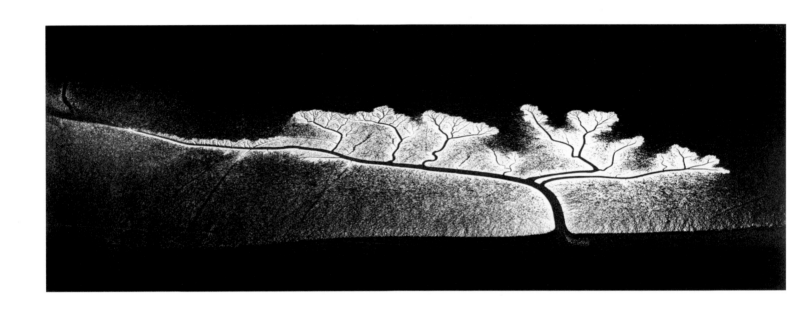

William Garnett

Reflection of the Sun on Dendritic Flow, San Francisco Bay, 1963/PRINTED LATER
Gelatin silver print

Ansel Adams

Aspens, Northern New Mexico, 1958/1978
Gelatin silver print

William Clift

Factory Butte, Utah, 1975
Gelatin silver print

The Urban Environment

Henri Cartier-Bresson

The Palais Royal Gardens, 1960/PRINTED LATER
Gelatin silver print

Wolf von dem Bussche

Foley Square, 1967/1980
Gelatin silver print

André Kertész
Untitled (Doorway, Budapest), 1924
Gelatin silver contact print

Max Yavno

Cable Car Turnaround, San Francisco, 1948
Gelatin silver print

Arthur Ollman
Untitled (Checkerboard Drive, San Francisco), 1977
Ektacolor print

Edward Serotta

University Library, Sarajevo, August 1988, 1988
Gelatin silver print

Edward Serotta

University Library, Sarajevo, November 1993, 1993
Gelatin silver print

James Pitts

World Trade Center through Branches, 1998
Palladium print

Karl Struss

Lower Broadway, New York, 1912/1979
Platinum print

Sheila Metzner

Chrysler Building (From Life), 2000
Platinum print

The Human Condition

Luis González Palma

Flores de Papel (Paper Flowers), 1990s
Hand-painted gelatin silver print

Jack Spencer

Man with Fish, Como, Mississippi, 1995
Toned gelatin silver print

Jack Spencer

Gussie's Magnolia, La Grange, Tennessee, 1997
Toned gelatin silver print

Don McCullin

Shell Shocked Man, Hue, Vietnam, 1968/1997
Gelatin silver print

Shelby Lee Adams

Berthie Napier with Pipe and John, 1992
Gelatin silver print

Lisette Model

Woman with Veil, San Francisco, 1975
Gelatin silver print

Heinrich Kühn

Two Girls, CIRCA 1905
Gum bichromate print

Manuel Alvarez-Bravo

Retrato de lo eterno (Portrait of the Eternal), CIRCA 1935/1980
Platinum print

Dolores Marat

La Femme du Musée Grevin, 1988
Fresson print

Nudes

Ruth Bernhard

Perspective II, 1967/1996
Platinum print

Jan Saudek

I'm Landing, 1984
Gelatin silver print

Edmund Teske

Big Sur, Hot Springs, 1962
Gelatin silver print

Brassai (Gyula Halasz)

At Susy's, Introduction, 1932/1976
Gelatin silver print

Andrew and Stuart Douglas

Matthew, 1993
Platinum print

Joyce Tenneson

Suzanne, In Contortion, 1990
Cibachrome print

Edward Maxey (Edward Mapplethorpe)

Maryanne, 1990
Gelatin silver print

Animals

Bettina Rheims

Pelican, 1982/1999
Gelatin silver print

Valerie Shaff

Carlo Aloft, 1996
Sepia-toned gelatin silver print

Bill Brandt

Evening in Kew Gardens, 1930s/PRINTED LATER
Gelatin silver print

Keith Carter

Sleeping Swan, 1995
Gelatin silver print

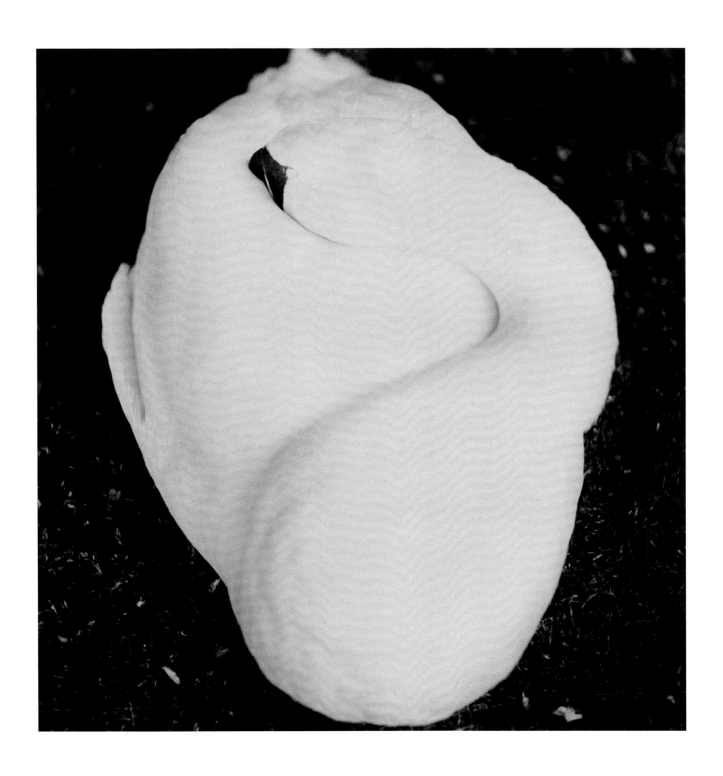

David M. Spear

Lee Neugent and His Puppy, 1992
Gelatin silver print

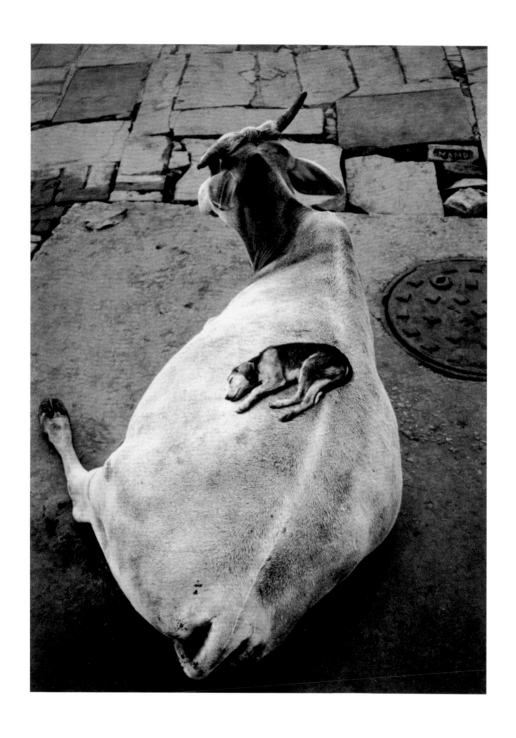

Pentti Sammallahti

Varanasi, India, 1999
Toned gelatin silver print

Still Lifes

Mark Citret

Quince, 1997
Gelatin silver print

Horst P. Horst

Vase with Flowers, Oyster Bay, 1989/PRINTED LATER
Platinum/palladium print

Rod Cook

FP #21 (Mushrooms), 2000
Platinum print

Laura Gilpin

White Iris, Colorado Springs, Colorado, CIRCA 1926
Platinum print

Cy DeCosse

Queen of the Night, 1998
Platinum print

Cy DeCosse

King of the Night, 1999
Platinum print

Robert Mapplethorpe

Allium and Bird of Paradise, 1979
Gelatin silver print

David Halliday

Durian Fruit, 1997
Toned gelatin silver print

John Blakemore

Tulipomania, No. 2, 1994
Gelatin silver print

The Modernist Impulse

Linda Butler

Spiral Staircase I, Pleasant Hill, Kentucky, 1982
Gelatin silver print

Imogen Cunningham

Leaf Pattern, 1929/PRINTED LATER
Gelatin silver print

Clarence John Laughlin

Receding Rectangles, 1942/1981
Gelatin silver print

Herbert Bayer

in search of times past, 1930s/1969
Gelatin silver print of photomontage

Arno Rafael Minkkinen

Self-Portrait, Fosters Pond, 1989
Gelatin silver print

Michal Macku

Gellage No. 53, 1992
Gelatin silver print

Vilem Kriz

Visible Woman with Butterfly Face, Berkeley, 1977
Toned gelatin silver print

Dominic Rouse

Man Eaten Alive by Chest of Drawers Whilst Searching for a Missing Sock, 1996/2001
Gelatin silver print

Jerry N. Uelsmann
Untitled (Sky Box), 1980
Gelatin silver print

Franco Salmoiraghi

Angel of Choice, 1995
Gelatin silver print

Exhibition Checklist

Berenice Abbott
United States, 1898–1991
Exchange Place, c. 1930/PRINTED LATER
Gelatin silver print
13⅞ x 3⅝ IN. (35.2 x 9.2 CM)

Berenice Abbott
United States, 1898–1991
New York at Night, 1932/1960s–1970s
Gelatin silver print
13¼ x 10⅝ IN. (33.7 x 27.0 CM)

Ansel Adams
United States, 1902–1984
Moonrise, Hernandez, New Mexico, 1941/1978
Gelatin silver print
15 x 19 IN. (38.1 x 48.3 CM)

Ansel Adams
United States, 1902–1984
Aspens, Northern New Mexico, 1958/1978
Gelatin silver print
20 x 15 IN. (50.8 x 38.1 CM)

Shelby Lee Adams
United States, born 1950
Berthie Napier with Pipe and John, 1992
Gelatin silver print
14½ x 18½ IN. (36.8 x 47.0 CM)

Manuel Alvarez-Bravo
Mexico, 1902–2002
Retrato de lo eterno (Portrait of the Eternal), c. 1935/1980
Platinum print
9⅜ x 7 IN. (23.8 x 17.8 CM)

Diane Arbus
United States, 1923–1971
A Woman with Her Baby Monkey, New Jersey, 1971
Gelatin silver print
15⅛ x 14 IN. (38.4 x 35.6 CM)

Tom Baril
United States, born 1952
Ranunculus, 1996
Solarized gelatin silver print
34 x 26 IN. (86.4 x 66.0 CM)

Herbert Bayer
Born Austria/active United States, 1900–1985
in search of times past, 1930s/1969
Gelatin silver print of photomontage
9 x 13¼ IN. (22.9 x 33.7 CM)

Herbert Bayer
Born Austria/active United States, 1900–1985
self-portrait, 1932/1969
Gelatin silver print of photomontage
13¼ x 10⅜ IN. (33.7 x 26.4 CM)

Edward J. Bellocq
United States, 1873–1940
Untitled (Seated Prostitute Wearing Mask), c. 1912
Gelatin silver print
6½ x 4½ IN. (16.5 x 11.4 CM)

Ruth Bernhard
Born Germany 1905, active United States
Perspective II, 1967/1996
Platinum print
9 x 15½ IN. (22.9 x 39.4 CM)

Ilse Bing
Born Germany/active United States, 1899–1998
Untitled (Tree on Île St. Louis), 1932
Gelatin silver print
11¼ x 8¾ IN. (28.6 x 22.2 CM)

John Blakemore
England, born 1936
Tulipomania, No. 2, 1994
Gelatin silver print
14½ x 19½ IN. (36.8 x 49.5 CM)

Bill Brandt
England, 1904–1984
Evening in Kew Gardens, 1930s/PRINTED LATER
Gelatin silver print
13½ x 11½ IN. (34.3 x 29.2 CM)

Brassai (Gyula Halasz)
Born Hungary/active France, 1899–1984
Bijou au Bar de la Lune, Paris (Miss Diamonds), 1932/PRINTED LATER
Gelatin silver print
14 x 10½ IN. (35.6 x 26.7 CM)

Brassai (Gyula Halasz)
Born Hungary/active France, 1899–1984
At Susy's, Introduction, 1932/1976
Gelatin silver print
11½ x 8½ IN. (29.2 x 21.6 CM)

Wynn Bullock
United States, 1902–1975
Graveyard Fence, 1948
Gelatin silver print
8 x 10 IN. (20.3 x 25.4 CM)

Linda Butler
United States, born 1947
Spiral Staircase I, Pleasant Hill, Kentucky, 1982
Gelatin silver print
14 x 11 IN. (35.6 x 27.9 CM)

Harry Callahan
United States, born 1912
Eleanor, Chicago, 1949, 1949/PRINTED LATER
Gelatin silver print
9¼ x 8⅜ (23.5 x 21.3 CM)

Robert Capa (Andrei Friedmann)
Born Hungary/active United States, 1913–1954
Loyalist Soldier, Spain, 1936/PRINTED LATER
Gelatin silver print
9½ x 14 IN. (24.1 x 35.6 CM)

Keith Carter
United States, born 1948
Lost Dog, 1992
Gelatin silver print
15 x 15 IN. (38.1 x 38.1 CM)

Keith Carter
United States, born 1948
Sleeping Swan, 1995
Gelatin silver print
15 x 15 IN. (38.1 x 38.1 CM)

Henri Cartier-Bresson
France, born 1908
Place de l'Europe, 1932/PRINTED LATER
Gelatin silver print
14 x 11 IN. (35.6 x 27.9 CM)

Henri Cartier-Bresson
France, born 1908
The Palais Royal Gardens, 1960/PRINTED LATER
Gelatin silver print
14 x 9¾ IN. (35.6 x 24.8 CM)

Mark Citret
United States, born 1949
Quince, 1997
Gelatin silver print
4½ x 4 IN. (11.4 x 10.2 CM)

Larry Clark
United States, born 1943
Pregnant Woman Injecting Heroin, 1971/PRINTED LATER
Gelatin silver print
11¾ x 17¾ IN. (29.8 x 45.1 CM)

William Clift
United States, born 1944
Factory Butte, Utah, 1975
Gelatin silver print
14 x 19 in. (35.6 x 48.3 cm)

William Clift
United States, born 1944
Portrait #5, Juan Hamilton Sculpture, 1978
Gelatin silver print
13 x 10 in. (33.0 x 25.4 cm)

Rod Cook
United States, born 1947
FP #21 (Mushrooms), 2000
Platinum print
19 x 15 in. (48.3 x 38.1 cm)

Imogen Cunningham
United States, 1883–1976
Magnolia Blossom, 1925
Gelatin silver print
7¼ x 9¼ in. (18.4 x 23.5 cm)

Imogen Cunningham
United States, 1883–1976
Leaf Pattern, 1929/PRINTED LATER
Gelatin silver print
12 x 9¼ in. (30.5 x 23.5 cm)

Cy DeCosse
United States, born 1929
Queen of the Night, 1998
Platinum print
23½ x 19 in. (59.7 x 48.3 cm)

Cy DeCosse
United States, born 1929
King of the Night, 1999
Platinum print
23½ x 19 in. (59.7 x 48.3 cm)

Robert Doisneau
France, 1912–1995
Le Regard Oblique (Sidelong Glance), 1948/1981
Gelatin silver print
9½ x 12 in. (24.1 x 30.5 cm)

Andrew and Stuart Douglas
England
Torso, 1993
Platinum print
19¾ x 15¾ in. (50.2 x 40.0 cm)

Andrew and Stuart Douglas
England
Matthew, 1993
Platinum print
19¾ x 15¾ in. (50.2 x 40.0 cm)

Elliott Erwitt
Born France 1928, active United States
New York (Dogs and Legs), 1946
Gelatin silver print
9 x 13⁷⁄₁₆ in. (22.9 x 34.1 cm)

Walker Evans
United States, 1903–1975
Lunchroom Buddies, New York City, 1931
Gelatin silver print
8½ x 7 in. (21.6 x 17.8 cm)

Arthur Fellig (Weegee)
Born Austria/active United States, 1899–1968
The Critic, 1943
Gelatin silver print
10½ x 13⅛ in. (26.7 x 33.3 cm)

Robert Frank
Born Switzerland 1924, active United States
Mary, 1955
Gelatin silver print
13⅝ x 8⅞ in. (34.6 x 22.5 cm)

Lee Friedlander
United States, born 1934
Canal Street, New Orleans, 1968/1981
Gelatin silver print
7¼ x 9½ IN. (18.4 x 24.1 CM)

William Garnett
United States, born 1916
Reflection of the Sun on Dendritic Flow, San Francisco Bay,
1963/PRINTED LATER
Gelatin silver print
6⁷⁄₁₆ x 19⁹⁄₁₆ IN. (16.4 x 49.7 CM)

Laura Gilpin
United States, 1891–1979
White Iris, Colorado Springs, Colorado, C. 1926
Platinum print
10 x 8 IN. (25.4 x 20.3 CM)

David Halliday
United States, born 1958
Magnolia Leaf and Seed Pod, 1995
Toned gelatin silver print
7 x 15 IN. (17.8 x 38.1 CM)

David Halliday
United States, born 1958
Durian Fruit, 1997
Toned gelatin silver print
25 x 25 IN. (63.5 x 63.5 CM)

Philippe Halsmann
Born Latvia/active United States, 1906–1979
Marilyn Monroe (Life *Cover Variant),* 1954
Gelatin silver print
14 x 10½ IN. (35.6 x 26.7 CM)

Horst P. Horst
Born Germany/active United States, 1906–2000
Vase with Flowers, Oyster Bay, 1989/PRINTED LATER
Platinum/palladium print
23½ x 19½ IN. (59.7 x 49.5 CM)

Lotte Johanna Jacobi
Germany, 1896–1990
Head of a Dancer, Berlin, c. 1929/PRINTED LATER
Gelatin silver print
8 x 10 IN. (20.3 x 25.4 CM)

Yousuf Karsh
Born Armenia/active Canada, 1908–2002
Georgia O'Keeffe, 1956/PRINTED LATER
Gelatin silver print
19¾ x 15⅞ IN. (50.2 x 40.3 CM)

André Kertész
Born Hungary/active France, 1894–1985
Untitled (Doorway, Budapest), 1924
Gelatin silver contact print
1½ x 2 IN. (3.8 x 5.1 CM)

André Kertész
Born Hungary/active France, 1894–1985
Paul Arma's Hands and Glasses, Paris, 1927
Gelatin silver contact print
3 x 3¾ IN. (7.6 x 9.5 CM)

André Kertész
Born Hungary/active France, 1894–1985
At the Animal Market, Quai St. Michel, Paris (Boy with Puppy), 1927–1928
Gelatin silver print
13¾ x 10¾ IN. (34.9 x 27.3 CM)

Vilem Kriz
Born Czechoslovakia/active United States, 1921–1994
Visible Woman with Butterfly Face, Berkeley, 1977
Toned gelatin silver print
13¼ x 10¼ IN. (33.7 x 26.0 CM)

Heinrich Kühn
Germany, 1866–1944
Two Girls, c. 1905
Gum bichromate print
12⅞ x 15⅝ IN. (32.7 x 39.7 CM)

Clarence John Laughlin
United States, 1905–1985
Receding Rectangles, 1942/1981
Gelatin silver print
15½ x 19 IN. (39.4 x 48.3 CM)

Danny Lyon
United States, born 1942
Cotton Pickers, Texas, 1968/1980
Gelatin silver print
13¼ x 18½ IN. (33.7 x 47.0 CM)

Michal Macku
Czechoslovakia, born 1963
Gellage No. 53, 1992
Gelatin silver print
26½ x 20 IN. (67.3 x 50.8 CM)

Robert Mapplethorpe
United States, 1946–1989
Allium and Bird of Paradise, 1979
Gelatin silver print
14 x 14 IN. (35.6 x 35.6 CM)

Robert Mapplethorpe
United States, 1946–1989
Lucy Ferry, 1986
Platinum emulsion on linen canvas
23¼ x 18¾ IN. (59.1 x 47.6 CM)

Dolores Marat
France, born 1944
La Femme du Musée Grevin, 1988
Fresson print
32 x 24 IN. (81.3 x 61.0 CM)

Edward Maxey (Edward Mapplethorpe)
United States, born 1960
Maryanne, 1990
Gelatin silver print
29 x 29 IN. (73.7 x 73.7 CM)

Don McCullin
England, born 1935
Snowy the Mouse Man, Cambridge, c. 1960/PRINTED LATER
Gelatin silver print
9⅛ x 13⅜ IN. (23.2 x 34.6 CM)

Don McCullin
England, born 1935
Shell Shocked Man, Hue, Vietnam, 1968/1997
Gelatin silver print
19¾ x 14 IN. (50.2 x 35.6 CM)

Sheila Metzner
United States, born 1939
Chrysler Building (From Life), 2000
Platinum print
22 x 18½ IN. (55.9 x 47.0 CM)

Arno Rafael Minkkinen
Born Finland 1945, active United States
Self-Portrait, Fosters Pond, 1989
Gelatin silver print
20 x 24 IN. (50.8 x 61.0 CM)

Lisette Model
Born Austria/active United States, 1906–1983
Woman with Veil, San Francisco, 1975
Gelatin silver print
19½ x 15¹¹⁄₁₆ IN. (49.5 x 39.9 CM)

Barbara Morgan
United States, born 1900
Martha Graham, Letter to the World, 1940/1972
Gelatin silver print
15½ x 19 IN. (39.4 x 48.3 CM)

Wright Morris
United States, 1910–1998
House in Winter, near Lincoln, Nebraska, 1941/PRINTED LATER
Gelatin silver print
10½ x 13½ IN. (26.7 x 34.3 CM)

Arnold Newman
United States, born 1918
Igor Stravinsky, 1946/PRINTED LATER
Gelatin silver print
10⅛ x 18⅞ IN. (25.7 x 47.9 CM)

Arthur Ollman
United States, born 1947
Untitled (Checkerboard Drive, San Francisco), 1977
Ektacolor print
13½ x 19½ IN. (33.7 x 49.5 CM)

Paul Outerbridge
United States, 1896–1958
Untitled (Compote with Fruit), 1922
Platinum print
4½ x 3⅜ IN. (11.4 x 8.6 CM)

Joshua Mann Pailet
United States, born 1950
Untitled, 1974, New Orleans, 1974/1983
Gelatin silver print
12⅜ x 18¼ IN. (31.4 x 46.4 CM)

Luis González Palma
Guatemala, born 1957
Flores de Papel (Paper Flowers), 1990s
Hand-painted gelatin silver print
19 x 19 IN. (48.3 x 48.3 CM)

Malcolm Pasley
England, born 1956
Peony, 1994
Platinum/palladium print
20 x 16 IN. (50.8 x 40.6 CM)

René Pauli
Switzerland, 1935–1999
Landscape No. 26 (Mission District, San Francisco), 1990
Tricolor carbon print
12½ x 15¾ IN. (31.7 x 40.0 CM)

Irving Penn
United States, born 1917
Cuzco Children, 1948/PRINTED LATER
Platinum/palladium print
19⅝ x 20⅝ IN. (49.8 x 52.4 CM)

James Pitts
United States, born 1953
World Trade Center through Branches, 1998
Palladium print
2⅛ x 2¹/₁₆ IN. (5.4 x 5.2 CM)

Neil Reddy
England, born 1963
No. 7 from the Series, "Three Feet to Infinity," 1995
Gelatin silver print
23⅜ x 18⅛ IN. (59.4 x 46.0 CM)

Neil Reddy
England, born 1963
No. 10 from the Series, "Three Feet to Infinity," 1995
Gelatin silver print
23⅜ x 19¼ IN. (59.4 x 48.9 CM)

Bettina Rheims
France, born 1952
Pelican, 1982/1999
Gelatin silver print
20⁹/₁₆ x 17⁵/₁₆ IN. (52.2 x 44.0 CM)

Dominic Rouse
England, born 1959
Man Eaten Alive by Chest of Drawers Whilst Searching for a Missing Sock,
1996/2001
Gelatin silver print
17¼ x 13⅞ IN. (43.8 x 35.2 CM)

Josephine Sacabo
United States, born 1944
El Final, 1997
Gelatin silver print
19 x 15 IN. (48.3 x 38.1 CM)

Franco Salmoiraghi
United States, born 1942
Nude on Rock, Yukie, 1978/PRINTED LATER
Gelatin silver print
14 x 14 IN. (35.6 x 35.6 CM)

Franco Salmoiraghi
United States, born 1942
Angel of Choice, 1995
Gelatin silver print
18¾ x 18¾ IN. (47.6 x 47.6 CM)

Franco Salmoiraghi
United States, born 1942
Cherye and Jim Pierce, New Orleans, 1999
Gelatin silver print
20 x 16 IN. (50.8 x 40.6 CM)

Pentti Sammallahti
Finland, born 1950
Solovki, White Sea, Russia, 1992
Gelatin silver print
5⅞ x 14¹⁄₁₆ IN. (14.9 x 35.7 CM)

Pentti Sammallahti
Finland, born 1950
Varanasi, India, 1999
Toned gelatin silver print
6¾ x 4⅞ IN. (17.1 x 12.4 CM)

August Sander
Germany, 1876–1964
Untitled (Man with Pipe), 1930/1950s
Gelatin silver print
11 x 8 IN. (27.9 x 20.3 CM)

Jan Saudek
Czechoslovakia, born 1935
I'm Landing, 1984
Gelatin silver print
11⅞ x 12½ IN. (30.2 x 31.7 CM)

Rocky Schenck
United States
Dresden, 1996
Toned gelatin silver print
16½ x 23 in. (41.9 x 58.4 cm)

Edward Serotta
United States, born 1949
University Library, Sarajevo, August 1988, 1988
Gelatin silver print
15 x 12¼ in. (38.1 x 31.1 cm)

Edward Serotta
United States, born 1949
University Library, Sarajevo, November 1993, 1993
Gelatin silver print
12⅞ x 12⅞ in. (32.1 x 32.1 cm)

Valerie Shaff
United States, born 1956
Carlo Aloft, 1996
Sepia-toned gelatin silver print
15 x 15 in. (38.1 x 38.1 cm)

Aaron Siskind
United States, 1903–1991
Jerome, Arizona, 1949/printed later
Gelatin silver print
18⅛ x 13⅜ in. (46.0 x 34.0 cm)

W. Eugene Smith
United States, 1918–1978
Spanish Village Spinner, 1951/printed later
Gelatin silver print
22½ x 17¾ in. (57.1 x 45.1 cm)

David M. Spear
United States, born 1937
Lee Neugent and His Puppy, 1992
Gelatin silver print
17 x 20½ in. (43.2 x 52.1 cm)

Jack Spencer
United States, born 1951
Man with Fish, Como, Mississippi, 1995
Toned gelatin silver print
17½ x 17½ IN. (44.5 x 44.5 CM)

Jack Spencer
United States, born 1951
Gussie's Magnolia, La Grange, Tennessee, 1997
Toned gelatin silver print
25½ x 25½ IN. (64.8 x 64.8 CM)

Edward Steichen
Born Luxembourg/active United States, 1879–1973
In Memoriam, 1904/1960
Gelatin silver print
12¾ x 10 IN. (32.4 x 25.4 CM)

Edward Steichen
Born Luxembourg/active United States, 1879–1973
Cheruit Gown, 1927
Gelatin silver print
9½ x 7½ IN. (24.1 x 19.1 CM)

Alfred Stieglitz
United States, 1864–1946
Flatiron Building, 1903
Large-format photogravure
13⅞ x 6 IN. (35.2 x 15.2 CM)

Paul Strand
United States, 1890–1976
Abstraction, Porch Shadows, Twin Lakes, Connecticut, 1916
Gelatin silver print
13⅛ x 9 IN. (33.3 x 22.9 CM)

Karl Struss
United States, 1886–1981
Lower Broadway, New York, 1912/1979
Platinum print
4⅝ x 3⁹⁄₁₆ IN. (11.8 x 9.1 CM)

Joyce Tenneson
United States, born 1945
Suzanne, In Contortion, 1990
Cibachrome print
13 x 10½ in. (33.0 x 26.7 cm)

Edmund Teske
United States, 1911–1996
Big Sur, Hot Springs, 1962
Gelatin silver print
13 x 10½ in. (33.0 x 26.7 cm)

Jerry N. Uelsmann
United States, born 1934
Untitled (Sky Box), 1980
Gelatin silver print
15 x 19 in. (38.1 x 48.3 cm)

Ron van Dongen
Born Venezuela 1961, active United States
Dahlia, "Jessie G.," 1998
Gelatin silver print
20 x 16 in. (50.8 x 40.6 cm)

Wolf von dem Bussche
Germany, born 1934
Foley Square, 1967/1980
Gelatin silver print
15½ x 22 in. (39.4 x 55.9 cm)

Brett Weston
United States, 1911–1993
Furniture Detail, 1925
Gelatin silver print
4½ x 3⅝ in. (11.4 x 9.2 cm)

Brett Weston
United States, 1911–1993
Canal, Holland, 1973
Gelatin silver print
9½ x 7½ in. (24.1 x 19.1 cm)

Minor White
United States, 1908–1976
Song without Words #2, c. 1947
Gelatin silver contact print
3⅝ x 4½ IN. (9.2 x 11.4 CM)

Joel Peter Witkin
United States, born 1939
Angel of the Carrots, 1987
Gelatin silver print
14½ x 14½ IN. (36.8 x 36.8 CM)

Eric Yanagi
United States, born 1952
Untitled (Black Man with White Baby) from "Waikiki" portfolio, 1973/1983
Gelatin silver print
8¹⁵⁄₁₆ x 13 IN. (22.7 x 33.0 CM)

Max Yavno
United States, 1911–1985
San Francisco—Mission Area, c. 1940s–1950s/PRINTED LATER
Gelatin silver print
7½ x 13½ IN. (19.1 x 34.3 CM)

Max Yavno
United States, 1911–1985
Cable Car Turnaround, San Francisco, 1948
Gelatin silver print
16 x 15½ IN. (40.6 x 39.4 CM)

Photography Credits

Berenice Abbot. *New York at Night.* © Berenice Abbot/Commerce Graphics Ltd., Inc., NYC.

Ansel Adams. *Aspens, Northern New Mexico.* Photograph by Ansel Adams. Used by permission of the Trustees of The Ansel Adams Publishing Rights Trust. All Rights Reserved.

Herbert Bayer. *in search of times past.* © 2003 Artists Rights Society (ARS), New York / VG Bild-Kunst, Bonn.

Bill Brandt. *Evening in Kew Gardens.* © Bill Brandt/Bill Brandt Archive Ltd.

Henri Cartier-Bresson. *Place de l'Europe; The Palais Royal Gardens.* © Henri Cartier-Bresson/Magnum Photos.

William Clift. *Factory Butte, Utah.* © William Clift 1975.

Imogen Cunningham. *Magnolia Blossom; Leaf Pattern.* © Imogen Cunningham/Imogen Cunningham Trust.

Robert Doisneau. *Le Regard Oblique (Sidelong Glance).* © Robert Doisneau/Rapho.

Andrew and Stuart Douglas. *Matthew.* The Douglas Brothers.

Walker Evans. *Lunchroom Buddies, New York City.* © The Walker Evans Archive, The Metropolitan Museum of Art.

Laura Gilpin. *White Iris, Colorado Springs, Colorado.* © 1979 Amon Carter Museum, Fort Worth, Texas. Bequest of the artist.

Philippe Halsman. *Marilyn Monroe (Life Cover Variant).* Photo by Philippe Halsman © Halsman Estate.

Horst P. Horst. *Vase with Flowers, Oyster Bay.* Horst Estate.

Yousuf Karsh. *Georgia O'Keeffe.* © Yousuf Karsh.

André Kertész. *Untitled (Doorway, Budapest); At the Animal Market, Quai St. Michel, Paris (Boy with Puppy).* © Estate of André Kertész.

Vilem Kriz. *Visible Woman with Butterfly Face, Berkeley.* Courtesy the Estate of Vilem Kriz.

Heinrich Kuhn. *Two Girls.* © Estate of the artist/Courtesy Gallery Kicken Berlin.

Clarence John Laughlin. *Receding Rectangles.* © The Historic New Orleans Collection.

Robert Mapplethorpe. *Lucy Ferry; Allium and Bird of Paradise.* © The Robert Mapplethorpe Foundation. Used with permission. Courtesy A+C Anthology.

Arno Rafael Minkkinen. *Self-Portrait, Fosters Pond.* © Arno Rafael Minkkinen.

Barbara Morgan. *Martha Graham, Letter to the World.* © Barbara Morgan, Barbara Morgan Archive.

Wright Morris. *House in Winter, near Lincoln, Nebraska, 1941.* © 2003 Center for Creative Photography, Arizona Board of Regents.

Luis González Palma. *Flores de Papel (Paper Flowers).* Represented by Benham Gallery, Seattle, Washington.

Bettina Rheims. *Pélican de profil, Août 1982, Paris.* © Bettina Rheims.

Dominic Rouse. *Man Eaten Alive by Chest of Drawers Whilst Searching for a Missing Sock.* Represented by Benham Gallery, Seattle, Washington.

Jan Saudek. *I'm Landing.* © Jan Saudek (www.saudek.com).

Edward Steichen. *Cheruit Gown.* Reprinted with permission of Joanna T. Steichen.

Alfred Stieglitz. *The Flatiron Building.* Alfred Stieglitz Collection, The Art Institute of Chicago.

Karl Struss. *Lower Broadway, New York.* © 1980 Amon Carter Museum, Fort Worth, Texas.

Edmund Teske. *Big Sur, Hot Springs.* © Edmund Teske Archives, Nils Vidstrand / Laurence Bump, Los Angeles, California.

Max Yavno. *Cable Car Turnaround, San Francisco, 1948.* © 1995 Center for Creative Photography, The University of Arizona Foundation.